Gratitude…

Thank you to everyone that was a blessing and nightmare. Thank you to those that were a guiding light and a destructive distraction.

Growing up Fatherless, provided acute knowledge of life. None stands out more than striving toward the ability to "…meet triumph and disaster and treat those two imposters just the same".

Peace,

FATHERLESS-The Conception

"When I was a child, I spoke as a child, I understood as a child, I thought as a child…" 1 Corinthians 13.

I thought my father was there. I knew his full government name. Seeing him rarely was enough to remind me I wasn't created in a laboratory. But that is all I knew; I only knew that I existed. The first piece in this exploration of being Fatherless was created when I was 15 years old. This was after waking, accepting my father left me 10 years prior. Believing in something has the power to sustain you, until that belief system crumbles. This early abandonment was constant in my life, yet I was able to mask it with perfection.

Why did Dad Leave

MOM, "WHY DID DAD LEAVE?" The man who has engendered me doesn't exist in my life. Is this man my father or just another man in the world? What is a father? This is a question I can't give a response to. I know father by definition, but personally I know not. I have seen pictures of myself as a toddler, and my "father" who I will call Stranger. I can only imagine through the pictures the happiness Stranger brought me. The pictures give me the image he was in a delighted mood. If only I could see the real picture, that can tell me the real story. I have a couple of blurry images that the pictures can bring back. Not of Stranger, but of the surroundings I've witnessed with him.

As an elementary student, I can recall boasting about Stranger. Having a smile thinking of Stranger. Whenever someone asked me about him I would say he lived in New Jersey, not knowing truly where he lived. During my fundamental learning, I remember seeing Stranger at his place of work. Once on a school trip I told everyone with pride and enthusiasm he was my father. Once when I was with my mother and cousin. This particular time I recall acting passive, as if I saw him on a daily basis. Just saying hello and going back to where my cousin was. My mother then hugged him and had a brief conversation with him. In my childhood that conversation never meant anything to me. As I grew I began to remember and wonder, what was said that last time I was ever in the presence of the father the stranger.

Through the next stage of my life, I began feeling an attachment to my stepfather. I began calling him my dad until he made me angry. Then, Stranger was my father. So now I had two fathers, one I saw daily and another I hadn't seen in a few years. My non-biological father gave me his heart in his hands. My biological father didn't even give me a word to pretend like he cared. Then my mom chose to be alone, so I was left with no home father. I still called my stepfather my father for a time. As time dwelled I no longer cared about him. I didn't want to know how he was nor did I want to be involved with him. My mom raised me from birth and that was all I needed. I now had no father when people asked of my stepfather or of Stranger. I was no longer confused of who my father was or who I was supposed to give my love to. That love never found a home, but each day it finds its way closer to my mom and no one else.

Now I begin to wonder where Stranger is and what he is doing. I meditate on Stranger coming back and my life, beginning over. So far, Stranger has not shown his face in my life. As I have grown I begin to ask of him and can get no positive response. No information that can lead me to Stranger. Stranger is lost in time and can't be found. Is Stranger dead or did he fall into the blackhole of earth. What did mom talk to him about at his job long ago? Why aren't our hearts in unison?

I need answers and help with millions of topics. The first thing I need answered is "Why did Dad leave?" The time, the waiting, all I can do is wait. What will happen to me? Will this empty void ever be filled? I don't know. I will never know anything anymore. For my heart, there will never be peace, never feel love again. The space for love is still there and will always stay. This love is eternal love that I will always feel towards Stranger.

My life needs help, it needs Stranger's help. Yet and still Stranger is lost, lost in body and soul. I need Stranger, but the same affection is not shared toward me. Now it is time to find Stranger for my heart needs to be fulfilled.

The investigation has begun. The investigation that will let my soul rest even before death. My mother, aunt and I have begun the search, to uncover what was lost in time. This investigation may take an eternity of heartbreaks. Being close but never there. Always that depressing step behind. Now I will be at an equal level if not a step ahead. Added to our equation will be a manhunter. To track Stranger down, so when he steps we will know.

FATHERLESS | The Conception

When Stranger retires for the night we will know. Know everything, no matter how acute or obtuse. When Stranger takes his final step, when he is about to die, should I kick Stranger in his heart to aid the cause? Should I feel this way about Stranger? Should I feel any love or hate towards Stranger? My mother and I begin to search. What am I searching for? Am I searching for a reason for love, for an eased heart? I don't know.

The blackhole in my heart and mind needs to end. I need to be saved from the horror of being ignorant of part of myself. My aunt, a police officer, has tried to help me come to peace with myself. She has tried to locate Stranger for months, that feels like years. Through networks of computers Stranger has become lost in a deeper hole. Hidden, behind an endless wall, not even the mighty computer can find Stranger. My aunt still and never will give up the search for Stranger. She loves me and cares about my feelings. My aunt is feeling the pain that I feel from not being able to be associated with Stranger.

How can I, a mortal compared to a computer, be able to locate the missing link? That piece of the chain stops my world from moving. The junction that stops the train from moving. The key that keeps the door locked. I need the key no matter how concealed it is. I will discover the key in my crazed world. Mother, mother is my heart and soul. Mother, the only person that has made me whole. Father, father has ripped, and tore at my heart and soul. Father has never been there for me to feed the fire of my love energy.

Stranger is my father, but not my father. "Father", should I even say that foreign word? All it means to me is pain, indescribable pain. Now it is time to surrender to this pain. Now it is time to surrender this pain, become free from this depression.

Dearest Me

Dearest Me.
Deep breath.
You are more than what you seem.

Dearest Me.
Stop right here.
Realize you are what you were made to be.

Dearest Me.
Close your eyes.
Those old daydreams, now they're reality.

Dearest Me.
Pause and consider,
Remember when the next opportunity was a
dream.

Dearest Me.
Be grateful.
Everything you asked has been laid for you.

Dearest Me.
Time to celebrate, turn around, reflect, watch,
Those grinding footsteps.

Reminding Me of Me

Innocence fleeing.
Losing perspective.
Waiting for substance.
Addictive reminiscent.
Focused on being free.
Just let me be me.

Dimmed light.
Shaded destiny.
Presently grieving.
Transposing seasons.
Cannot feel complete.
You're not with me.

Radioactive feeling.
Cemented to the ceiling.
Paralysis reaching.
Depths of infinity.
Pit of desperation.
Darkened me.

Resurrection.
Anticipating elevation.
Confused similarities.
Deepened sanctity.
Enlisted in fantasy.
Reminding me of ME.

Shadow I Cast

Not as strong as the shadow I cast.
Easy to spout off important things that last.
Pitching suggestions and allegations
relentlessly.
But those soliloquies don't inspire me.

Not as influential as the wake of success.
Trained in the art of war, only pursued the sure
victory.
Encouraging every soul within my grasp.
But that inspiration doesn't care for me.

Not as thoughtful as gracious people say I am.
I'm avoiding regret and karma on the back end.
Making a difference in other people's life.
But life isn't the same for me.

Not as caring as I care to be.
Able to ignore desperate people in time of
need.
Selfishly focused like that doesn't impact me.
But it's who I am.
And that person is me.

Just Being Me

Always hear promises of what life could be.
Never ever seen it turn into reality.
Lots of vain words.
And repetitive rhetoric about a future that will
never be.
I'm good just being me.

Every time I go around the sun.
Someone alluding to what has just begun.
I get the positivity, but it doesn't mean shit
without sincerity.
So, I just keep it moving, head on a swivel,
cause my reality is I'm good just being me.

Sitting here. Laying here. Staring here.
Thinking here.
Lying in a devastating reality of a fucked up
fantasy.
Youth ain't even here to protect my ego.
Just here with a frustrated libido.
Just need more practice letting go.
I'm good just being me.

Self-preservation and self-interested
commitments being made as cool as sitting in
the shade. It's just an illusion to convince
people that the resolution would benefit
someone not just about getting paid.
So, I stay focused.
I'm good just being me.

Finding the peace called serenity.
To be alone in a crowd of people.
That peace of mind of being able to use every
piece of time.
Just being me.

Prayers For Me

William G Bryant Grandfather of 7 birds, in his
own words.
The King led us to one vision Family for life.
But when he lost his life so did the vision.
What meant more to me.
There was always a prayer for me.

Land is all you got in this world.
You have to defend it until the end.
But in the end we squabbled
over who would make the decisions.
Couldn't manage, land abandoned, that was
the end.
There was always a prayer for me.

Always have somewhere to lay your head.
Make sure there is a woman to keep you fed.
Wasn't until I was years in,
I understood the wisdom of the sin.
There was always a prayer for me.

FATHERLESS | The Conception

Strong heralding voice reaching the heavens.
The whole house could hear.
Praying the sacrifices of predecessors would
guide me through the years.
Building in me such a worldly view.
There was always a prayer for me.

The lesson I learned is the lesson I give.
Speaking abundant life into my own kids.
Describing the Picasso of their life.
Enshrining in their soul that we only have one
life.
There was always a prayer for me.

There were no more powerful words as these "I
am proud of you grandson."
Before and after every single greeting.
Each talk.
Each walk.
Each ride.
Each day at the beach.
There was nothing stronger than King Bryant,
So blessed he put that strength in me.
There was always a prayer for me.

Who Knows Me?

Who knows me?
Walking this world with billions of people.
Yet I walk it alone.
No one could say they know my dreams.
No one can say they love me.
No one knows me.

Who knows me?
Cannot remember someone offered to help.
When was the last time I had a visit?
Have endless experiences but none were
momentous.
But I'm sure people have asked loving
questions.
And I casually find a way to deflect them.
The wall that protects me is strong.
No one knows me.

Who knows me?
There have been people seeking to find the
entry.
But I let no one in.
Blame everyone for the wrongdoing of a few
and that was the end.
There is no worth in loving unconditionally.
More misfortune than lies than any happy
feeling.
Take the easy way out and stay alone.
At least I know who I'm with.

Protect Me From Me

What would I be without me
Without the self-hate and self-doubt
How would I make it without
That negative energy that drives me
I pray, Protect me from me

Remember the tribulations
Feeling of the pain from separation
Avoiding the bullets final call
Left with nothing positive in me
I pray, protect me from me

The challenge of the remedy
Lack of belief that I can be better than me
Nothing wrong with where I am at
It's ok if I never reach the potential of my being
I pray, protect me from me

What's Left Of Me?

Disappointed in resentment
Unforeseen fulfillment
Understanding the resilience
Unequivocally connected to resistance
Progressing through darkness
Trudging past the loneliness
Creeping around uncertainty
What's left of me?

Envisioning upward awakenings
Aggravated into unfamiliar feelings
Resurrection of derivative viewings
Starting to think something new
Initiating a different point of view
Second guessing it's you
Unraveling this mystery
What's left of me?

Invoking this opening scene
Believing in the unknown things
Prayerfully accepting the unseen
Earth shaking the life outta me
Waves changing how I breathe
Thrust of windfall controlling my fall
Appreciation for something I can see
What's left for me?

Sun shining 360
World spinning feverishly
If I could get off

Where would I be
Fear got a hold of me
Devastated remembering the past
Shattered in how long it'll last
Lost in life definitely
What's left for me?

Hand

_____

Hand against my forehead
Wiping down my face
Trying to erase all this disgrace
Exhaling every past sin
If God is God
Why won't God exist in me

Hand on my lower back
Pushing out the stress
This world on my neck
Reaching for that medication
No help from any of these relations
They just assume expectations

Hand wiping my eyes
Surprised by these surprises
This mirror looking right into me
Recast in tears just scare me
Unexpected circumstances
There are no fair chances

FATHERLESS | The Conception

Hand gliding across my cheek
Trying to hide these tears
Been keeping them in for years
Uncontrollably controlling me
If I was who I was I'd never be me
Drowning in misery

Unwanted For So Long

I have been unwanted for so long
Only want people that don't want me
Lovely feeling chasing fake memories
Making beauty out of the worse things
If I ain't unwanted must be something wrong
Cause why would someone
Ever want to want me
Cause why would someone
Ever want to stop putting pain on me
Addicted to this pain
It's the only real thing

I have been unwanted for so long
Afraid to say my own name
It must be the initiation of this innermost pain
Magnetism embedded In the syllables
Pulls negativity directly into me
Sitting and waiting
Waiting and thinking
Thinking and listening
Listening and believing

FATHERLESS | The Conception

Believing in pain
Cause pain is what I know
So I keep it close to me

I have been unwanted for so long
Rorschach said to me
It makes me happy
I don't want to even see
That you stay hurting me
It's not you It's me
Situational silence
Violent surprises
Weight heavy for me
World won't wait for me
Will you bring it to me
That peaceful way
Loving me every day
Thinking it's a new way
When it's my only way

Sy Bryant   24

You Left Me Dad.

YOU LEFT ME DAD.
As a toddler you never gave me a chance to
say Da-Da, but I said Ma-Ma.
You never were there when I fell to tell me that
I don't need to cry, but mom was.

I realize Man is the opposite Woman, but is
Mother the opposite of Father? Everything
mom does, dad does not? Every day my mom
was there to give love, my dad was not.

WHERE WERE YOU...........?

Now I am a man, a father. I'm making money
and you're not. Now you need me, but I no
longer need you. You lost your life and mine
has just begun. You are now asking for my
love. My reply is "Hell No!".

I'm the bastard, but you're going to be treated
like one.

Childhood Ways

Cannot explain this hole in me
I open up the old photo albums from 1980
The smile looked real and sincere
But I do not ever remember that feeling being
there
It was just me and her for the longest
You stepped on the scene
Knew straight away
You were the strongest

I thought life was real
When y'all got married
And I got your last name
First party I remembered
At the Cornucopia
Everyone so thrilled
Dancing endlessly
Staying with family
As y'all drove away

Remember running up the steps
Saw you laying on the floor
I was scared to death
Crazy part is,
I was up to no good
Use to steal your coins
Just rebelling because I could
Thought you were gone
Ambulance arrived
You kept saying you were fine

FATHERLESS | The Conception

Everything suddenly collapsed in me
Read this letter
About how much you loved me
And how what is happening
Wasn't about me
Just something that couldn't be resolved
Those words they stung me
Wasn't even a year since the ceremony
Really thought you adopted me

Couldn't accept that you never left
Even got a house in walking distance
Still bear your last name
But it's not the same
Trying to explain to the seeds
My father is not their grandfather
You are not my father
Their grandfather is not my father
And they look at me like
I'm insane

Promised God at that point
Before I was even two digits around the sun
I would never give that feeling to my son
It created this burden in me
Breaking through stereotypical curses
So many unresolved emotions
So embedded In my psyche
Just to release it creates thousands verses

And I cannot to this day
Say I am healed from any of it

Sy Bryant   27

More like build up resilience
To all kinds of bullshit
Temper stays short and lit
Portray a light hearted laugh
Keep people real relax
But the gritted vengeance
Already considered how to end this

Demons

___

Got so many demons
Of shit
About people leaving
And shit
When people stay around
I'm out the shit

Only thing I'm use to
Is being alone
So when the house is full
It don't feel like home
Feeling alone just being me

People in my life
Stay reaching out
And if I knew they'd stay
I would reach on out
Reality different for me
Keeping distance
Plain as you can see

FATHERLESS | The Conception

Treat everyone
Based on the torture of the past
It's how I'm built
This wall will last
Got me before
Ain't happening no more

Hope

I still remember you from childhood days
That constant feeling you gave on Xmas days
Anxiety deafening every move that was made
That hope, that constant hope you made

You are always there in the strangest way
Regardless of how I feel, showed me the way
When you're not around I struggle to make
sense
Ambivalent traversing life like a 6th sense

Closed my eyes and see you there with pride
In the midst of the pain striving for that pride
The future of this abyss leaves me yearning
peace
Traversing this void no shortcut to this peace

Yet, I'm still here, energy drained, still need
more
Striving again to see you once more
I miss you, that newness, that hope

Sy Bryant   29

That anticipation, and realization, I need that
hope

Keep Writing

Keep writing
Just to get it all out
Anything I can do
Cannot scream and shout
But the frustration
It's confusing
The peace It's elusive

Keep writing
Speaking life into me
Somehow gaining energy
Constant serenity
Searching for more
Bless me with more
Always looking for
That gentle peace
Keep writing
Doing all I can
Letting it slip through
The anger, the fascination
Everything in me
Causing the hysteria
Rain drenching
Thunder rattling

Trying to Write It Out

If I could write out everything,
Maybe it would be something new to sing.
The stories of the past weigh on me.
Never found anyone to share with me.
Everyone wants me to solve their problems,
But what do I do about my problems?

Trying to write it out.
The pain.
Lost dreams.
Unfulfilled hope.
Small things.

Embarrassed for you to know,
Everything I do is not in control.
A lot of gut reactions,
Just so happens to turn out right for someone
else.
But for me, the gut reactions don't work.
Just endure day to day.

Trying to write it out.
The pain.
Lost dreams.
Unfulfilled hope.
Small things.

FATHERLESS | The Conception

Never had a good day in my life.
Moments of smiles since I was a child.
People promising fake beliefs,
The disappointment turned me really mean.
Now I cannot believe what people say.
People just say shit to get you out the way.

Trying to write it out.
The pain.
Lost dreams.
Unfulfilled hope.
Small things.

Cannot spend my whole life in complaints.
So, I just keep the train moving.
Pretending day to day,
Making people believe everything is ok.
Then I noticed people just accept what they
want to believe,
And what's really going on will remain unseen.

Trying to write it out.
The pain.
Lost dreams.
Unfulfilled hope.
Small things.

Sy Bryant   32

Waiting

Waiting on the steps
From the dawn of light
Anticipating the excitement
From last night
Plans was made
Times agreed
Made sure I was washed up
Ate up
Ready for anything

Dawn turned to day
Way before pagers and smartphones
Ringing the house
No one was home
Patiently waiting
Mom tryna convince me
It's better to wait inside
So afraid to miss my ride
Just counted the cars go by

Day turned to evening
Friends coming back
Full day of sweating and playing
Asking if I'll go for round 2
Nah, I said I was waiting for you
Continued to wait
Excitement in me
Every-time I saw
Car lights slow down momentarily

Sy Bryant   33

FATHERLESS | The Conception

Evening gave way to night
Crickets starting
Lighting bugs now visible
Steps my anchor
Misery my crucible
Mom says you just called
That you apologize
You'll make it up
First time I no longer gave a fuck

Night turned into a new day
Kept tryna to think
What did I do
Why didn't you come get me
I was good all week
Got all my work done
You promised to be there
I didn't know lying was acceptable
Maybe I was just gullible
New day turned into New Year's
Same little promise
But now I know
As plain as I can see
Your words and actions don't mean the same
thing
We was never the same
Always saw you differently
Never again wanted that excruciation

Rejected Being

Woke up crying
Mom asked why
I cannot remember the dream
I remember
Not wanting to be alive
Why did he leave
I just never knew
Mom said
This is what I will do for you
I will reach out to him
Because he owes you this
She ended with a kiss

The time was arranged
The phone did ring "hello"....
Tears was all I could bear
He waited for a while
With a lisp he asked, "Are you there?"
From his point of view
I didn't need anything
My mom would provide it all
Thus the burden was past to me
Would I leave my children,
like he left me

Children arrived one at a time
After a while I started to understand
It isn't easy to be a father, to be a man
I reached out again
Just one more time

Arranged a visit sporadically
Ended up in his home for the night
Not necessarily comfortable
But just something I needed to do
Even saw pictures of my "nephews"
With the same dimples that my two have
Regardless of individual feelings
Genetics are still passed

That was the end of that chapter
We connected a few more times
Nothing significant
Just no longer had any interest
But somehow that one scene
On the Fresh Prince of Bel Aire
It still gets to me
Will asks Uncle Phil
"Why doesn't he want me?"

Love Of Pain

The pain
It is so routine
When it flickers a bit
Dissolved in an instant
What does it mean?

Held it closely
Personally guarded secret
Smiling easily

Sy Bryant   36

FATHERLESS | The Conception

Behind closed doors
Feeding the beast

Waking up in laughter
Strangely irrelevant
Searching for the pain
I do readily accept it
Now I'm left indebted

Opening curtains
Feeling the morning gaze
Mind is unlimited
Seeing the new day
Anchors aweigh

The shadow lures me
The comfort of darkness
No witnesses to witness
The marvelous emotion
That love of pain

FATHERLESS - The Realization

There's a phrase that I have heard the majority of my life, "the truth will set you free" -- John 8:32. I absolutely believe this, but this belief doesn't mean it is emotionless. Pain and truth are sometimes synonymous, and for some it is the reason we would rather not discuss the truth. I was not able to process many early emotional barriers. As a result, I kept reliving moments and events that were just moments in time and should have been treated as such.

Half Of Me

Half of a person
Since I sensed my conscience
That is the view of myself
Even through every blessing
Very sheltered upbringing
There is a hollow being
Knowing the origins of
Only one side of me

Half of myself
Over the years
Sporadically learning genetics
Understanding, even without interaction
Resembling a stranger's actions
Left in a sea of doubt
Sorting manly feelings
Without evidence of those feelings

Half of me
Enjoyed every minute in isolation
Latch Keyed in
Just me and pets as friends
Rainy days the epitome of loneliness
Not a real person in sight
Now I seek solitude
Even if I need to be rude

Half of everything

Sy Bryant

The concept is equivalency
Hormones and chromosomes
Creating a new being
Conceptually perpetuating
Every good quality of individuals
With only one side lived as if I already dead
Half of it
Glad I had it
Every sacrifice she made for me
Every dollar she wasted on me
Every cry she comforted
Regardless of the love I had
Nothing can replace wanting a dad

Ever Been Alone

Alone in this room
Since yesterday around noon
If the law of attraction is real
What does it mean when
When there's no one to feel

Have you ever been alone
In that place by yourself, alone
No one to call, alone
No one to see, everyone is gone
Only thing left is.... being alone

FATHERLESS | The Realization

Thoughts flowing freely
Lot of people say they need me
But in the fell clutch of circumstances
By myself, defiant
With no more chances

Have you ever been alone
In that place by yourself, alone
No one to call, alone
No one to see, everyone is gone
Only thing left is.... being alone

Every so often I meet a new face
Dare not open up in that place
Cause I know what I bring
But always hesitant
When I hear the same game

Have you ever been alone
In that place by yourself, alone
No one to call, alone
No one to see, everyone is gone
Only thing left is.... being alone

I know in the end I'll be ok
Cause time heals uncertainty
Need faith to hold straight
So Ima hold on
This ain't nothing new
I will keep on

Sy Bryant

Have you ever been alone
In that place by yourself, alone
No one to call, alone
No one to see, everyone is gone
Only thing left is.... being alone

I don't stay down for long
I take a little time just to mourn
Each day is something new
But I know
I know
I will get through

Growing Up

Growing up
I thought love was forever
Remembering every image
 It's like, embedded in me
Now I'm left wondering
Feeling so empty
Was it all an illusion
Crazy ideology
Cause I've never thought
It was all within me

Growing up
I thought happiness was a place

FATHERLESS | The Realization

Everything we did had a space
As time keeps moving
Feel like I'm losing my place
Stuck in a space
Where I have lost my pace
So I quietly assume
That we in the same place
So I already lost the race

Growing up
Consumed in things
I could never really fathom
Luxurious items
Thought I needed to have them
Ended those dreams
Cause they weren't worth a thing
Striving for materiality
But that don't mean a thing
Staying focused on nothing

Growing up
Caused me all kind of grief
Kept believing in people
That could care less about me
Reaching levels of anxiety
Everything felt real
But it was all just a dream
Losing my insight
Let the truth behold me
Lost the fight

Self-Reflect

It's hard not to self-reflect
Based on where I am today
Deepened into curiosity
Of each choice that I made
Trying to alleviate myself
The doubt and pain
Consistently leveraged
To bury myself

Self-reflection
More than a mirror will ever show
Rewinding for a moment
Specific situations
Even a few examinations
Trying to fathom the impossible
That I rewrite history
Curse of an unconquerable soul
Reflecting on my past self-Circumventing each time
I did the right thing
In the right time
Because I negatively
Don't want to be me
So I constantly re-evaluate
How I came to be

Perpetrating my own reflection
Applying filters readily

FATHERLESS | The Realization

Unknowingly maintaining
That morbid view of reality
Neglecting the higher calling
Of why I am the way I am
Ungrateful in my own satisfaction
Just a passenger in the inception

Reflection retrospectively
The numerous assurance
I offered in individual pursuits
Believing they are happy,
Enjoying every bit of life and liberty
Cause those fantasies ain't for me
Created realistic fantasies
That conspired and paralyzed me

Comfort

Comfort in repetition
Signs of deeper trouble
Repeating repetitively
As if something is easy
Do not have to worry
About things with new meaning

Comfort in tradition
Hides everything in everyone
Doing the same things
We are all accustomed to
Discomfort is overshadowed
Hidden in costumes

Comfort in holidays
Instead of the present
Reminder of better days
Evident in the daily ways
Application of statistics
Systemic anomalies

Comfort in history
Accepting the burdens of reality
Recognizing you left
As someone left you
Yet you were unwilling to stop
What was done to you
Comfort in ignorance

I don't even know you
After circling the sun for decades
Your name is an illusion
Your existence embodies confusion
Never understand why you created me

Depth

Depth of eternity
Discover my sanity
Peace ignores me
Evaded positivity
Attracting empty

Darkness surrounding
Doubt engulfing
Downwardly pressing
Inevitably breaking
Brace destroying

Hope dissolved
Freedom evolved
Faith concentrated
Love incinerated
Light faded

Striving bounty
Screaming loudly

Sy Bryant   47

Brightening cloudy
Thinking profoundly
Standing proudly

What Am I Doing Here

What am I doing here
What have I done
All the blessings
Given to me
Yet I still long for one
That peace of serenity
That prayer of Jabez
Bring me home at last

What am I doing here
What will become
Decisions that should have been made
I ignored them with ignorance
Choices I should have made
Took for granted they would always be there
Yet here I am
Wondering where I am
What am I doing here
What is yet to be
When I look up into the sky
I do not see what I'm meant to see
All I see is a reflection of me

Every doubt and sacrifice
Feeling the weight of it on me
Questioning was I meant to be

What am I doing here
Was this life even meant for me
Looking around
Realizing that no one is around
Moving through the shadow's protections
Supporting unreciprocated emotions
Truths rarely spoken honestly
World full of people, yet it is just me

Foundation

Foundation is cracked
Repairs have been attempted
But like any infrastructure
Built on the wrong premise
Only way to fix it is destroying it
The impossibility of resurrection
Is the only thing that kept me
From just hitting reset
If I could just start all over again
The things I'd do differently
Or not even start at all
If I had a conscience at that point
Avoid that egg
Give it my all

Foundation been nurtured

FATHERLESS | The Realization

Many a craftsman
Observing the damage
Understanding the weeds
Strangling the fruit
Until it's unraveled
Planted and nurtured
But without question
Would turn and Walk away
Thinking at least the garden is clean
Unknowingly creating another crack
Nothing changed really
Just lost a bit of confidence actually
Knowing that look that is given
No time to correct it, stay off track

Foundation with some blemishes
Like having a beautiful painting
That leaves no image
Everyone creating in their own mind
The true meaning of it
Seeing obsolescence easily
Yet walking away so freely
As if they weren't the architect
Not theirs to repair
Just as easy to neglect
Motherhood is a feeling Fatherhood is a choice
Chosen over for so long
Lost my voice

Foundation weakened
Bridge stays ready to collapse

Sy Bryant

FATHERLESS | The Realization

Indeterminate frequency
Sent crashing to my knees
Could be the smallest of things
Child's poor performance in school
Major catastrophes Of car accidents
Releasing everything I can no longer hold within
And the crumbling
The holes open wider
Slowly without cessation
Causing moral degradation

Foundation strengthened
Through periodic episodes
When peers see me at my worst
They elicit in me the beat in me
Purple skies we discuss
Until the early hours
When the golden rays
They light the way
Remembering I got this far
Battered torn and all
Fault lines that have made some fall
Still here aiding in the mission
No time to wallow in regret
Go until I have nothing left

Desperate Attention

Yearning solitude
Pursuing anyone
Irrelevant person
Desperate attention

Selfish attitude
Invaded peace
Limited proximity
Desperate attention

Affiliated quiet
Grappling affection
Irresponsibly loving
Desperate attention.

Sheltered anxiety
Intimate desires
Instantly gratified
Desperate attention

Vulnerable

I am completely exposed
Floating around space
Not comfortable in any place
Replaying history
Dramatic mystery
Knowing it got me
Overtaken History's fear

I am completely empty
Void of energy
Nothing sustains me
Striving toward endless hope
Watching the swinging rope
Seeing the end
Painless Present's gift

I am completely envious
Life has no justice
Being in this body's life
Cemented in strife
Longing for longevity
Life's brevity pleasing me
Searching Future's hope
I am completely ending
Hope stays evading
Earth spinning without me
Harmful destiny
Latching onto love

Wherever love finds me
Loving Living eternally

The Night…

The night is my worst enemy,
With its shadows of mystery
Trying to get me.
The darkness knows
All that I am,
Seeing me strong and weak,
Always in constant watch
Tempting me
With that wicked energy.

The night is the only way to the sun.
Yet hides the way for patience sake,
Nothing more could be done.
Waiting to wait.
Anticipating the sun's rays,
Hoping light will show a new way
Away from this dark retreat.

The night and me have nothing but contempt.
We know each other's moves,
Yet we never go further than distant associates.
A head nod is all that's exchanged,
As night hints

It's time for you to get out the way.

The night stills the world.
To rest.
To become new.
The night moves suns shadows and focus
Causing me to lose focus.
The night
The tranquility of the unseen,
Nothing is visible
And it's serene.

All Wrong

Expecting the wrong things
Going down the wrong roads
Wondering wrong thoughts
Lost on wrong paths
Or So it seems

Seeing wrong visions
Having the wrong dreams
Absorbing the wrong nourishment.
Believing in the wrong light
Or So it seems

Hoping for the wrong future
Knowing the wrong individuals

Sy Bryant   55

FATHERLESS | The Realization

Hearing the wrong songs
Driving to the wrong destinations
Or So it seems

Choosing the wrong interactions
Focused on the wrong goals
Rejuvenating in the wrong fuel
Dumping in the wrong pool
Or so it seems

Grinding on the wrong work
Saving the wrong people
Sacrificing the wrong time
Believed in the wrong soul
Or So it seems

Shadow Created

This breeze
Blowing through a blue sky day
No clouds
With slow memories
Drifting past my way
Years of days
Traversing this earth
Concentrated on bad decisions
Indecisions
Wondering
How much was truly taken from that circumcision

Raising youths In the shadow I created
Moving life indiscriminately
So they avoid things that I hated
Constant belief
Experiences
Knowledge
Won't be enough
At some point
They will face life
Life
In its tumultuous phases
Bringing triumph and disaster
With multiple faces

Fighting through
Perceptions

FATHERLESS | The Realization

Of generational legacies
Finding that
One ray of sun
With unlimited possibility.
Learning through experience
My history as their base
Praying
Their seeds
Are planted in a new place

The vision is clear
Success near
The joy upon their dimpled cheeks.
It is just that
Moment of peace
That I'm longing to seek
Striving for tomorrow's sun
To witness
Us stronger
Then when this day began

Make It Last

Sitting here thinking about the past
I'm always surprised
I was able to make it last
It ain't an anchor
But a lot of lessons learned
Now I'm just tryna
Heed my own words

Just never knew I'd end up here
Filled with all kinds of shit
I don't want to hear
Thinking of the present future
With the past right here
If only you knew
If only I could bear

Walking this street
With the rain falling
Screaming out loud
And it's God I'm calling
I need to understand
Why I'm being punished
Who did I hurt
What did I do
Feeling like I'm finished

Just never knew I'd end up here
Filled with all kinds of shit

FATHERLESS | The Realization

I wouldn't even want to hear
Thinking of the present future
With the past right here
If only you knew
If only I could bear

Think I'm scared
To know the truth
What would be revealed
If I knew the truth
Contemplating shit
That ain't even real
Caught up in past decisions
Like it's my final deal
What am I supposed to do?

Just never knew I'd end up here
Filled with all kinds of shit
I don't want to hear
Thinking of the present future
With the past right here
If only you knew
If only I could bear

Just Different

Experiencing things Differently
As if different choices were made
Imaging the differences as reality
Now I'm stuck on this fantasy
What "Ifs"????
And If "That's"....
None of it means a thing
In reality It's not better or worse
It's just a different path
To the same thing

Going deep into the emotion of different things
Plotting out new courses
With a different ring
The difference of this emotion
Is only
That I'm trying to make it different
Like trying to only
Carve out the best
Like this fantasy
Won't let me rest
Repeating my past
With different decisions
Precisely laid out
Like an incision
It's just a different way
But the same pain

Sy Bryant   61

FATHERLESS | The Realization

Looking at money differently
Don't need different banks
To exchange pennies
I am the hedge fund,
Creating wealth differently
Money
Watching money
Make money
Different life sure to be
That different life
Different expenses surely
And in an instant
Still broke as could be
But at least I made the money Differently
Pain is soothed by different thoughts
As if I weren't in control
The first time around
The different things
I would have done
If and only if
I knew what I know now
Same intelligence
Doesn't lead to a different result
This is the life I have
I could start living
Or be lost
Focusing on where I am
Versus where I thought I should be
The only difference
Is the difference
I claim to be

Misunderstanding

Never understood anything you did
There are times I wanted to understand
The education that you gave
Conquering the body and emotion
With fierce devotion
Never heard a word of love
Just a Hey periodically
Never a call or even a visit
Just now
Trying to figure out what I was missing

Definitely remember
The few interactions
Weighed heavy enough
Never wanted to get any closer
Extremely comfortable with closure
Driving 80 miles per hour
Sharp curves
Gliding graciously
Because no point in driving
If you are doing it soberly

Fairly ambiguous about many things
There was so many times
That your name didn't mean a thing
Just a joke of sorts
As the pipe was lit
All I really recall was that first hit

FATHERLESS | The Realization

It didn't sting,
it burned,
lash of that belt
Because of the effort you gave
Just another bit of abuse
From a man that knew me from the very beginning
Even when I knew
You were leaving the earth
There was nothing left to experience
Nothing new for us to review
Just heard about it in passing
Do not remember shedding a tear
Ashes stored in a closet,
like trash on a shelf
Knowing that you would no longer be here
It was in that moment that I truly learned
The value of life on this earth

Living In This Fantasy

Living in this fantasy
Got me thinking differently
Stay considering if it weren't fiction
What level of complacency
Would get a grip on me
Removing possibility of reality
Just to Settle down

Living in this fantasy
Birds harmonize with the breeze
Sweetest song I've ever heard
Don't even understand a word
Aligning with a new frequency
People passing by consider envy
Arms outstretched accepting energy

Living in this fantasy
Absorbing the raw sincerity
Mindfully trusting in insecurity
Blinded through
Undetermined fate
Sureness invading every space
As if this was real I would be surreal
Living in this fantasy
Inadequacies growing within
Germinating from the outside in
Destroying my sensibilities
Left with nothing but hesitancies

Admiring realism
From a fantastic view

6th Sense

Just now understood the 6th sense.
Everything just started making sense.
Seeing life with a fictional lens.
Non-Fiction doesn't always end driving a Ghost.

Living in my fantasy life.
Kept thinking happiness materialized if I had a wife.
Wanted to believe in mystical things.
Thought prayer and hope led to beautiful things.

The sense of the 6th degree.
Woke me up to reality.
People are going to be who they are.
Don't believe in people's words shit don't go far.

It's a blessing to wake up from the dream.
Tired of the tears hiding the scream.
Seeing life in a new direction, a stronger focus.
Knowing what's important without emotion.

That 6th sense was the answer, so it seems.
Remembering the past as a stranger.
Things I thought, I know I didn't really see.

FATHERLESS | The Realization

I just imagined shit that would never be.

Eyes wide open the truth hurt
No one to blame that's the shit that really hurt
Looking in the mirror, like, is you insane?
Purposely hurting yourself like you don't know your name.

Heard It

Heard it said
A few times
That it was better
Without a father
No one to disappoint you
No one to live up to
Started to believe it
It was a way through it
But this hole in me
It says something different

Heard it mentioned
I have a good life
Not associated with
Any negative statistics
Fluid opportunities
To be whatever I want to be
Travel endlessly
It's like saying

FATHERLESS | The Realization

I am full
But never had anything to eat
Things are different for me

Heard it discussed
I am blessed
God's most valiant of soldiers
Endured hardships
Never would have imagined this
If I acted on the hate, would I be remiss?
Just imagined thoughts
Trying to end these feelings
Like imagining what you see of me
Means that I am happy

Heard it trivialized
Do you need a specific gender in your life?
Isn't love enough to conquer bounds?
Is happiness only accumulated by opposites?
Individually we can achieve anything.
Success is only a plateau to the beginning.
I readily get all that theory
But only two people created ME
One I know and love, the other left me empty

Lost So Much ….

Lost so much, but still have everything
Only possible losses are material things
Remember seeing people transition
The mystery is revealed in everything
King Bryant proclaimed with thunderous sound
As long as you say my name I live.
So now I say it every day accepting he is still with me
Recognizing I was mourning
Future memories
I didn't even see

Lost so much, but still have everything
Only possible losses are material things
Growing up with that key round my neck
That shit wasn't easy for me
Big as I was, not even two digits yet
Walking past all kinds of mess
Nothing to do at home but create fantasy
Realized I wasn't lonely, just was being me
But I damn sure guaranteed
My seeds wouldn't go that way

Lost so much, but still have everything
Only possible losses are material things
Grew up with so much I was giving it away
Thinking these little trinkets were in the way
There was a whole world to see
But I was so busy enjoying being me

FATHERLESS | The Realization

Meeting social expectations I ventured out
found out what the world was about
Saw I wasn't missing a thing, but me

Lost so much, but still have everything
Only possible losses are material things
Seeing distress from different points of view
From nicotine, from alcohol, sex, narcotics
From fixing cars, fixing the yard, painting new paint
People doing anything to avoid what life brings
I saw a bunch of people out in this world
Trying to find that solitude that I released
Laughing at the psychology of my disbelief
We are all missing the opportunity to be me

FATHERLESS - The Damnation

My maternal grandmother's name is Elizabeth McCrea Bryant. She would embed all types of phrases in our life. None stuck with me more than "it gets by degrees." Living in this life, each year has felt more complicated and more grueling. There was no particular moment or instance that was of significant importance, yet the world felt so heavy. Consistently trying to help others reach their goals and potential, while never focusing on myself. I was just not that important.

Opening A New Day

Opening a new day
Sun ain't shining my way
Look of frustration upon me
Where do I get reciprocity
All the sins, jaded history
Expecting that I'd be worthy
For the sun to shine on me

Opening a new day
Nothing happy near me
Realizing blame exist
Sadness can no longer resist
This tear I created
Wishing away
Turmoil I created

Opening a new day
Looked up and stared
Just running away
There was no mistaken
This feeling I've taken
Internalized this within me
Heartache eternal destiny

Opening a new day

FATHERLESS | The Damnation

Same shit, different day
Habitually loving everyone
There is no love for me
Enduring mixed fantasy
Living in this social reality
Real reality too much for me

Trusted You

Realizing that people leave
Counting the leavers
Really surprising
Unrecognizable arrivals
Creating fake families
Believing everyone
Is loving everyone
Latching onto
Familiar surroundings
Create environments
Where trust is digested
Completely accepted

Realizing that people are cruel

FATHERLESS | The Damnation

Animalistic natural evolved us
Yet never leaves us
We selfishly elate in individuality
Seeing differences seems normal
Watching individuals become immoral
Enabling the self-centered being
To become the only thing that matters
Ignoring the existence of other beings
Gratification
The highest pursuit
Hate everything about you
Overtly enabling the deadly sins

Pressed into silence
Surprisingly ignored it
Didn't know the intricacy
Challenging to explain things
Just realized my explanation
Didn't mean a thing
I mean the realness wasn't received
How important is language
Context changes every meaning
Suddenly the loneliness
The experience rebirth in me
Seeking solace desperately
Burden is heavily applied
Tears from years of the same cry
Built the foundation internally

Most significant item
The only thing I hold onto
Holding this relentlessly
Trust no one completely

Years Of Tears

Years of tears
Letting every drop
Build up
Hold it in
Containing it
Letting evaporation
Evaporate every sin
Take away each pain

Years of tears
The dam is well maintained
Always with
A smile on the face
Hiding every disgrace
Left thinking
How to hide everything
As if I don't feel a thing

FATHERLESS | The Damnation

Years of tears
In the pit of despair
Feeling the void
Lost energy
Everything leaving me
Any possibility to see
Something new
Old world view

Years of tears
And every few years
I release these tears
Flushing out everything
Lost in this belief
As if pain is temporary
Believing in this
No end to this

Never Met

Every promise I remember keenly
The deep rooted voice
That African American tone
Every promise with a smile
Engrained, fabricated with love
Explaining away idiosyncrasies
Promises need to cease

Every promise meant so much
Someone was listening
Felt like someone was asking
And these first few years
Just had people telling me
Mistakenly believing in me
Promises not for me

Every promise laid bare
There was a different tone
Whenever you were there
The joyous smiles that filled me
Smile or cry on cue
Did anything to avoid you
Promises were never you

FATHERLESS | The Damnation

Every promise digs deep
Pound of earth
Heaped on me
Started losing that purity
Started emulating what I see
Became fake, actor portraying me
Promises left me
Every promise promised more
Silence spoke for me
Lost every expectation
Of anything you had in me
Slowly moved toward my own way
Avoiding every reality the long way
Promises aweigh

Duality

Loved and rejected
Synonymously interwoven
Associate one with the other
As if they are one in the same
As I come to accept the real
Pain
Loving ones that reject you
Rejecting ghosts that love you

Peace and pain
Intertwined overtime
Pretending I'm at peace
With the pain within me
So comfortable in fact
Life
Is the peace
I feel in pain
The pain becomes my peace

Accepted and deteriorated
Building inescapable fate
Witnessing my own demise
Longing for an escape
Accepting the amount of hate
Existence

Sy Bryant   79

FATHERLESS | The Damnation

Accepting a deteriorating life
Deteriorating accepting systemic defeat

Hope and Hate
Creating mystical obstacles
Hoping for Love and Peace
Hating the pain and rejection
Deteriorating my acceptance
Living
Regardless of this past
Independently I shall last

All This Pain

All this pain
Stirring in me
People everywhere
Feeling So Empty
Joy please find me

Wide awake
New day's sun through this window
Barely touching me in misery
Trying not to move
Somber mood everything is ok
What I've learned to say
Tired of talking
Been thinking
Yeah I know what's wrong
Love got me blinded
Can't you see,
It's me

All this pain
Stirring in me
People everywhere
Feeling So Empty
Joy please find me

FATHERLESS | The Damnation

Phone vibrating
Been turned the ringer off
Know who it is know what they want
Ain't even worth the effort
To pick up the phone just want to be alone
Everyone think they can fix me
But I know they can't fix it
Cause I'm that one
That fix their shit
Counting out each day
That I've felt this way
Deepened hopeless mood
Yeah been kind of rude
Just not in the mood

All this pain
Stirring in me
People everywhere
Feeling So Empty
Joy please find me

Knocks at my door
Yelling who is it
Delivery especially for me
Probably another bill
Too many to count
To know for sure
Special box for me

FATHERLESS | The Damnation

Opened with energy
Just a note for me
Tears for my eyes
Old notes from my Grandfather
Miss him every day
Since he past
Reading the proudness
Giving me hopefulness

All this pain
Stirring in me
People everywhere
Feeling So Empty
Joy please find me

Need my ladder out
Climbing out of here
Breaking down
Walls of emotion
Initiating devotion
New plan developing
Open up this window
Fresh air welcoming
Getting new point of view
Pain in the rear view
Eyes focused on the future
Wounds finally closing faith is a suture
Optimistically looking

Sy Bryant   83

The joy life caused me
Strength resurrected within me

All this pain
It is me
All this joy
It is me
All this pain
All this joy
This pain
This joy

Love of Pain

The pain
It is so routine
When it flickers a bit
Dissolved in an instant
What does it mean

Held it closely
Personally guarded secret
Smiling easily
Behind closed doors
Feeding the beast

FATHERLESS | The Damnation

Waking up in laughter
Strangely irrelevant
Searching for the pain
I readily accepted
Now I'm left indebted

Opening curtains
Feeling the morning gaze
Mind is unlimited
Seeing the new day
Anchors aweigh

The shadow lures me
The comfort of darkness
No witnesses to witness
The marvelous emotion
That love of pain

Bastard Life

Recognized it quickly
Early on in childhood
Ninety houses on one street
I was one of the few
Where it was just My mom and me
It was clearly recognized
Just a different energy

Things that
Were significant for us
The relationship was based on trust
The mom had to provide
Meaning I saw her sporadically
When she was home
She was tired
From all the sacrifices for me
She would absolutely be there
For all those trivial things

From 5401 to 5491
Families upon families
We enjoyed our youth profusely
Individually everyone had their issues
But when we were together
We had no issues

FATHERLESS | The Damnation

But everything was different for me
Because in our crew
I was the one that had the curfew
The individual with the single parent home
Most of the day no one was home
No one to even get peace from
Dude was never there
It was just the challenge
I'm the only one that says "dad"
But when I say it
It has no meaning
No one responds
The air swallows it up
No one gives a fuck
I swore to myself, a solemn promise
I never was going to be that dude

Eventually I started labeling others
Calling them dad because I had none
Camp counselors, teachers
Any man I gave a crown to
Always had men in my family
But they weren't always around
And every man with the same belief
He'll be okay eventually
He's mom can do more than me

Signs were evident something was wrong in me

Sy Bryant

FATHERLESS | The Damnation

But not those normal Red flags you see
I wasn't in jail
Went to every class
Did exceptionally well
Teachers viewed me well
Mom provided everything
Supporting both of us
But now that festering of pain
Always feels like it will erupt
So accustomed to this feeling
Dare not disturb the feeling
Just keep ignoring the signs
Let them pass with time

Darkness Will Shine

The bottomless pit
That envy
Consuming mortality
Focused externally
Believing I'm not who I claim to be
Claiming another's destiny
Plotting over time
Darkness will shine

Expecting insanity
Repeatedly executing
Repetitiously anticipation
As if a different outcome
Will finally come
Unchanged methodology
The answer, unequivocally
Cannot be me
Darkness will shine

Preparation for abundance
Creating repositories
Futuristic inventories
Organized scheming
Suit and tie conspiracies
Eliminated electronic trails

FATHERLESS | The Damnation

Buried evidence
Resurrected above the skyline
Darkness will shine
Deeply contemplating this
Post mortuary visits
Explaining all the details
Limitations of statutes
Impermeable to virtues
Accepting final peace
You never knew it was me
Darkness will shine

Eternity

Eternity of vengeance
Lays beneath my skin
Absorbing every sin
Every situation I'm in
Gently gliding fluidly
Patiently feeling unity

Eternity of envy
Admiring possessive beings
Building their happiness
Creatively framing this

FATHERLESS | The Damnation

Projecting different opportunities
Anxiety of empty dreams

Eternity of forgiveness
Voided understanding
Impossibility treating you differently
Imagining you didn't damage
Awoke inner savage
Hardened into hatefulness

Eternity of kindness
Sweet summer breeze
Surf rising below your knees
Remembering the hatefulness
Accepting gracefulness
Rejecting the peace in this
Once or twice you can blame someone else
But when it's routine you got to blame yourself

Handle On Me

Hurting for so long
Self-inflicted
Rationalizing others effects on me
I cannot remember anyone staying with me
At some point everyone leaves
So eventually I would leave
Before they would leave me

Do not share the inner you
Having prescribed emotions
Reading people before they read you
Staying on the defense
Only trust to my own boundary
Cause I know it's just me
The mirror looking at me
And the only one it sees is me

Living four lives on a constant basis
The reality of the past
Wondering how long it'll last
The what if of the past
As if I could avoid my past
The fantasy of the future and presently
As if the previous three
Don't already have a handle on me

What Do You Do?

When it doesn't even hurt no more
Is there anything more
Taken in all sorts of the word
Taken for granted with every word
What do you do
When there's nothing else to do

When it doesn't even hurt no more
Every moment looking at the door
Every minute a choice to leave
Every second the guilt piled on me
What do you do
When all hope has left you

When it doesn't even hurt no more
Counting of the score
Of each and every "No"
My how rejection grows
What do you do
When there is no more left in you

When it doesn't even hurt no more
Disappointment is expected
After each and every rejection
Left in a state of awe

Sy Bryant   93

What do you do
When faith is done with you

Hollow Being

Emptied
The past relentless' pain
Trials and travesty
Nothing left in me
Hollow being

Hollow being
Transparently clear
Imperfections' solitude
Nothing holding me dear
Planted seeds anchored me

Watching wind blow
Feeling lights energy
Encapsulated in this human
Trapped by this cage
Hollow being
Hollow being
Witnessing life's curse
Living an unwilling life

Captured dreams
Real life tragedy

Never Knew

Never knew a day of love
Unless it was with a day of pain
Love makes you look at things
But with a different point of view
Start to believe in people
Believing in things
As if all of a sudden
All that talk that's been talked
Somehow it's supposed to
Suddenly come true.

Never knew a day of love
Unless it was with a day of pain
Not even sure what I'm seeing
Things look different with rain
Things so cloudy
Fog start blinding me
Pretending if I squint
Somehow I'll see things differently
Hoping if I just go to sleep

FATHERLESS | The Damnation

When I wake up
Things will turn out differently

Never knew a day of love
Unless it was with a day of pain
So engulfed in life
I shudder to even say my own name
No matter where I'm at
It's always a lonely thing
Because love told me
To be on guard for any possible thing
Therefore when I leave the house
I stay on guard
Watching and moving
Ready to turn out if caught off hard

Never knew a day or love
Unless it was with a day Of pain
The more I think about it
The more I feel it
The more I think
I need it
What is it that keeps me
What is it that's always with me
What will be there from start to stop
If not for pain
What would I even feel
Doing anything to stay away

Sy Bryant   96

FATHERLESS | The Damnation

Avoiding every opportunity
To end this pain In me

Never Letting Go

So long a part of me,
That now I find energy from misery.
It's a daily affirmation making and checking.
The gates and walls keep that hidden ghost hidden.
Muscle memory is stronger,
I can fight not much longer.
People impressed at the rudimentary shit I do,
Cause they don't know I'm never letting go.

Brick and mortar use to be torture.
As I had to modify techniques to remain unique,
So common enemies could go right past.
Without a thought of the hidden vulture.
Death constantly looming,
Watching my moves,
Wondering why I spent so many hours,
Protecting mental heirlooms.
Death didn't know I'm never letting go.

People keep mentioning this place that's free.

Sy Bryant   97

FATHERLESS | The Damnation

Speaking of earth like its really heaven.
If I could only see.
Each day that triumph and disaster,
I see completely changing destinies.
Wondering.... where is their fortress?
Where is their shield, how can they exist?
Not knowing how to manage life's unexpected tendencies.
What would they be if they really knew,
That I'm never letting go.

The past is the only teacher we have.
There is an illusion that there is good and bad.
The response to that which is gone is the changing fad.
A culture of social dictatorship enforcing how you must feel
and what you must do.
But what if, the answer is just in you.
Picking and choosing what to include and exclude not the
solution,
The mastery of managing the response is the revolution.
Never Letting Go.

Sleep Away The Pain

Sleep away the pain
Please allow me to be me
Escape this self-caused misery
Deepening in me
This PAIN Won't let me be
Embarrassing to admit it
Feeling convicted

Sleep away the pain
Longing for a time
Where peace is mine
Surrounded by opportunity
 PAIN let me free
Why can't I see a way
Without a complicated belief
Anything for a relief

Sleep away the pain
Without longing for toxins
Let sleep be my serenity
Closer than my own breath
PAIN won't let me rest
Gripping my inner being
Heart minimally beating
Don't even know what I'm seeing

Sy Bryant   99

Sleep away the pain
Reality proves me insane
Hoping that faith will set me free
Barely stay afloat in this
Why am I remiss?
Absorbing PAIN so closely
Lord please forgive my envy
Wishing pain wouldn't control me

Every Bit of Smile

Every bit of smile
Has left me
Voice lost its crispness
Slurring through
The last 24 hours
I've lost my power
Weakened into submission
Heart beating slower
Appetite much lower

Answering calls out of necessity
Hoping the natural rays
Find their way to be
Please give me the strength I need

Sy Bryant   100

FATHERLESS | The Damnation

Help me to just be free
Allowing plans to stay on track
Feeling so wasted
Inner peace is devastated I have nothing left

Feeling out of sorts
Not knowing where I am
Buried under layers
Fabric won't protect me
Just an illusion of confusion
Easier to wipe away the tears
Afraid that I must face
My deepest fears It's been years

Wondering if it's just me
Does anyone else feel me
Labored breathe leaving me
Vision unable to digest clearly
Energy is nowhere near me
Clouded by my own memory
Traveling this last mile
I've seemed to have lost
Every bit of smile

Defeat

Lightest struggles
Weighing heaviest
On my mind
All the time
I'm feeling invincible
Then I felt destructible
Following the last line.

Heaviest motivation
Leading lightly
Heard this politely
Everything that was real
It was really out of place
Thinking of the possibility
To get back on pace.

Smoothest mountains
Creating illusions
Had me believing In global evolution
Eradicated from hate
Perfect air and water quality
World's greed ended me

Roughest roads
Things never told

FATHERLESS | The Damnation

Focused on the outcome
All smiles, laugh for miles
With feet bare
Bleeding to the meat
Lost in shear defeat

Rain Keep Falling

Rain keep falling
Please just a while longer
Protect these tears
Creeping out of me
Touching my cheeks
Mix with precipitation
Keep hiding me

Rain keep falling
Holding this in for so long
Staring straight into the sky
Thunderous lightning passing me by
Releasing what holds me
Refusing to cry
Punishment stay coming out my eyes

Rain keep falling

FATHERLESS | The Damnation

Holding them for years
Counting every single tear
Falling each second
Struggling to wait a second
Calling out for strength
What am I missing?

Rain keep falling
Fall on me
You're the only one
That is supporting my need
Need to feel this and release this
Never lived without pain
Does that even makes sense

Unknown

This unknown entity
Never let go of me
Around 4 years old
Suddenly become old
Lost every sense of enjoyment
People stay wondering
What is it?

Event after event
Made it clear to me
The person I was meant to be
Guarded up, from the bottom up
Trusting few individuals
Remembering peoples potential
Friendship is essential

Give everyone
That first opportunity
To see if they can see me
Deciphering what is done
Interpretation of what is said
Whenever they don't match
The shit is dead

I never let it go

FATHERLESS | The Damnation

Remember it diligently
Can see the white walls
All around me
Not sure what was happening to me
Tiled ground felt uneasy
In just a few minutes youth was empty

Now I'm old
Bitter and heart so cold
Not forgetting or forgiven
The amount of time stolen from me
Heard you were dead
No empathy,
No Sympathy T
Thanked God for the peace mind
That is living in my head.

FATHERLESS - The Evolution

There are so many emotions we will feel in our lifetime. Feeling them in an instant is neither Right nor Wrong. Whether it is learned behavior or a means to manage the insanity of life, there is always a possibility to change that mental state. These thoughts are not new or planned out, but a recognition that those emotions must be released in a positive manner. Negativity seems to fester within us, until we are able to make Peace. Peace with what we've been through, Peace with who we are. Peace with our Evolution.

Praying

Prayed for rain,
Now I'm standing in mud.
Really thought I knew what I wanted.
It was dry and barren.
Thought I just needed to be caring.
Confidently I knew the way,
Now that rain drained my day.

Praying, For what I want.
Praying, For what I need.
Is praying the answer,
Or should I just wait patiently.

Prayed for strength,
Now I've lost my compassion.
Really thought if I could just be stronger,
I could make it last much longer.
Tears.
Heartache.
Now it's gone,
But so too is the passion.
Now I can't feel anything,
Just the weight of this strength upon me.

Praying, For what I want.

Praying, For what I need.
Is praying the answer,
Or should I just wait patiently.

Prayed and prayed,
But I'm still in need.
Got every single thing that I've prayed for,
Yet I'm empty.
Learning to accept and manage,
Instead of praying for greener grass.
It's all just an illusion, and this too shall pass.

Releasing

Releasing every thought
Each perspective
All ideas that contain
All the limitations
I have every experienced
The thoughts that prevent progression
The idea that is now a nightmare
Releasing it all in the crisp cool air

Releasing every limit

Sy Bryant   109

FATHERLESS | The Evolution

Thorn of thoughts
Piercing the flesh of forgiveness
Debilitating fruits of labor
Void of thought, is what I savor
Enabling the strength to succeed
That's all I really need

Releasing every history
Today is a new thing
Intentionally filling it with new dreams
Building ideas, concepts, pure energy
Interlocking joy with jeopardy
Risking it all on everything
Just to hear the birds sing

Releasing every goal
Built things on things that were old
Expecting something new seems bold
Sacrificing the intimate stories told
From now on, leave the past alone
Investing in what I can call my own
Free to be alone

First Tear

First tear gave way for another
Wallowed within the mystery
The deepest darkest scheme
Started as just a dream
Which enabled envy
Thinking I'm more than another

First tear washed away the fear
Created new opportunities
Opened every door I saw
Didn't realize this was all
Recognizing hopes improbabilities
The coldest day gripped in fear

First tear washing the past
Out the window staring
Seeing the intricacies
Peeping the mysteries
No one even caring
How long will it last

First tear just a shadow of me
Sun exaggerating the humidity
Sweat filling each and every pore
With infinite dollars I'm still poor

Slowly losing every bit of dignity
Void of everything I claim to be

Energy Gone

Heart beating slower
Mood much lower
Struggling to consume
No more room
Emptiness vastness
Prevailing blankness
Captured by darkness
Subtle tone
Energy gone

Looking deeply
Nights mystery
Reminding me
Endless possibility
Stars for me
Shining brightly
Stomach bonded tightly
Swift anxiety
Cannot move

FATHERLESS | The Evolution

Life disapprove
Flesh and bone
Energy gone

Cannot breathe
Pain underneath
Longing disbelief
Driving passion
Simple compassion
Lack of focus
Depressed diagnosis
Opening conclusions
Summarized illusion
Unanswered phone
Energy gone

Confusion

Confusion building me
Hearing intricacies so clearly
Imagination overpowering me
Distilling the real of reality
Mirror persecuting me

Confusion breathing me
Hesitating with each thought
Rethinking everything about me
Normally blaming what I was taught
Mirror persecuting me

Confusion becoming me
Focusing on intangibilities
Praying they avoid me
Believing in new realities
Mirror persecuting me

Confusion bewildering me
Devastating ideology of eternity
Expecting life infinitely
Ignoring the death of lividity
Mirror persecuting me

Confusion breaking me
Contemplating life's desires
Morbid reality of destiny
Entirely mortified fire
Mirror persecuting me

Days Long Gone

Time gone.
And every time the past comes to the present,
I can feel the present being wasted again.
That past is cemented in the deep caravans of the earth's
core.
There is nothing that can be done with days long gone.

Time alone.
In the midst of time, it stands alone.
Unstoppable.
Unforgiving.
I just need a single moment to allow the past pain to heal.
But you push me forward as if my pain is irrelevant.
There is nothing that can be done with days long gone.

Time free.
Never once paid for you,

But you are constantly in my life.
Each day I become more indebted,
Yet I never even asked for you.
I need freedom.
You've held me too long.
There is nothing that can be done with days long gone.

Time bound.
I cannot find peace.
You hold me so tightly I cannot see my next step.
And I struggle to even believe.
Why do you command my life so strongly?
Why cannot I just be I.
There is nothing that can be done with days long gone.

All I Have Is Tomorrow

All I have is tomorrow
Nothing left in me today
Wishing the earth moved faster
Cause today
The mirror showing me
All that I am
Lost in this space
Cannot find the race

All I have is tomorrow
Today is already spent
I've tried, and I've tried
Until I'm tired of tired
What other way could I go
Streets so quiet
Like feet against new fallen snow
Left with nowhere to go

All I have is tomorrow
Every plan has failed
Staring at the blueprint
Second guessing what heaven sent
Releasing what this world has meant
Slowly thinking, about the next step
Paralyzed in analysis

Still cannot figure out what I missed

All I have is tomorrow
Cannot even sleep
Waiting for the first hour to approach me
Laying out something deep inside me
Praying over this so I can believe in this
Patiently waiting for this evolution
Extracting the earth's energy in one revolution
Faithful, believing in a solution

Riding & Writing

Riding to a plateau
Just to feel that deep burn
Unable to focus on anything else
That deep burn turns to pain
And all I have to do is hold on
So I can release everything

Writing to a ghost
Expressing everything
What I love and hate the most
Allowing every anchor on me
To finally be free

FATHERLESS | The Evolution

Cause I cannot live
And be captive simultaneously

Riding to new heights
Wind grabbing me
Trying my best
Trying to push free
Absorbing all my energy
Exhausted breathing
Unfocused, Is my heart still beating?

Writing every word
Anything that comes to mind
Allowing any word
To make me sublime
Letting it flow through
No boundaries
No obstacles
Let it pass through

Death Comes Inevitably

And I'm running around
Crazily into the mystery
Pretending I can make
Something more of me
As if I can change
My family's legacy

And I'm watching
Life on this earth
Embedded in her hearth
Struggling to see clearly
Looking through mirrors
Cannot even see me

And I'm just moving
So slowly that the world
It's just spinning around me
Barely keeping up
Losing minutes
Lost time for me

And I'm thinking
Maybe this life It ain't for me
But I don't need to do a damn thing
Cause death comes inevitably

Sy Bryant   120

Of .... For .... In .... Peace

Gritting teeth in anger
The irritating grind
Consumed in this
Labyrinth of unachievable peace
Longing for existence
In the reminisce
Of the derivative of peace

Struggling feverishly
Treading for understanding
Overwhelming circumstances
Wondering if there is a peace
Searching constantly
Consistently pressing
Probing for peace

Slowly setting sun
As if the world just begun
Seeing life in your presence
Believing that there is a peace
Closing eyes gradually
Holding onto final memories
Reality exist in peace

Sun Left

Before the sun left
I gave all that I had left
No reason to hold on anything
Time is lost instantly
Income versus outcome
Irrelevantly becoming numb
Slowly accepting everything
Achieving nothing

Before the sun left
I gave away all that I had left
Holding onto material things
Draining potential of offspring
Suffering through differing thoughts
Searching for that ideal spot
Admiring the rear view
Blessed given all I've been through

Before the sun left
I started believing with all I had left
Hoping to see the next day
Mindful of obstacles coming my way
Seeking something innovative
Keeping this life in perspective
Launching ideas into the universe

Quitting is the only curse

Before the sun left
Lost all I had left
Riding into eternal abyss
Praying not to reminisce
Avoiding every pain of the past
Asking vehemently for it to pass
Slowly sinking from disgrace
Peace achieved in this final resting place

Serenity

Seeking serenity
Looking into every past
Each person touched
Every place with a tear
All the residual that was left

Asking serenity
Feeling the variability
Unlimited choices
So many missed steps
The past anchors me

Speaking serenity
Talking life into everything
Realizing pain instantly
Life not for me

Feeling serenity
Every breath precious
Each pulse exaggerated
Planted synergy
Infinite energy

Vision

The vision to see beyond my dreams
Random thoughts instantly appearing
Joyous laughter in the deepest pit of fear
Seeing an entire life in one idea.

The vision to believe past circumstances
Living for future realizations
Finding harmony throughout the turmoil
Viewing this world in just one peace.

The vision more than imagined
Being in the midst of elaborate fantasy

Guiding each breathe to reach elation
Awakening innate power of success

THEN & NOW

THEN...
I would hold onto everything
Analyze this until I paralyzed this
Seeking a conclusion
Before moving toward a solution
Endless internal debate
Stayed being late.

NOW...
I let it all go
Let it flow right through me
I don't even filter a thing
Let it all go through
Now I'm hearing
A new you

THEN...
I was trying to prove something
Looking for a chance to do something
Eagerly pursuing titles

FATHERLESS | The Evolution

Climbing for a different caste
Constantly reminded of reality
Landed right on my ass

NOW...
I move like the wind blows
Filling in where I am needed
I'm never impeded
Riding out suggestions
As if they are manifestations
Relaxed in elevation

THEN...
I had an expectation of others
Timely adhering to their word
Keeping commitments sincere
Holding onto everything I hold dear
Disappointed responses from me
Toward someone not wanting to be me

NOW...
I don't know you nor need to
I stay focused on me
And everything that I choose to be
Believing in inevitably of serenity
Avoiding happy and sad moments
To remain peaceful in the moment

Holding Nothing In

Hold nothing in
Portray it all out
Thespian my being
Off the cuff
Creating what I'm seeing
Adapting to scenery
Everywhere I am has meaning

Hold nothing in
Keep the pipes wide open
GRIEF, excitement, MISERY, elation, CONTENTMENT,
enthusiasm, MEDIOCRITY
It All runs Right through me

Hold nothing in
Keep grabbing endlessly
Plate getting too heavy
Too much to hold, got to fold
Heart turn cold
Realizing if it's for you
It won't benefit me

Hold nothing in
Sleep easy at night
Letting all this peace in

Not an ounce of hate
Smiling as the master of my fate
No more head swivel life
Once I got my peace right

Feeling The Thunder

Thunderous sky
Echoing across skin
Piercing into dreams
The days reckoning
Accelerating tomorrow's prayers
Bellowing sacred peace

Lighted sky
Clearing the night
Deepening glances
Mellowing earth
Engulfing serenity
Yearning soft soliloquy

Pounding rain
Hid every stain
Tears refreshing
Invoking joy desperately

Anger building
Love's healing

Gentle fog
Covering the earth
Hiding every footprint
Hiding each mistake
Every bit of energy
Awakening forgiveness

Hungry

Hungry
Never been hungry once
Had moments of discomfort
Reality provided comfort
Ensuring temporary uneasiness
Engulfed in envy
If I could just be hungry

Hungry
Plate indefinitely full
Generational sacrifices
Eating repeatedly easily
Granted taken desperately

FATHERLESS | The Evolution

Blessings absorbingly
If I could just be hungry

Hungry
Growling deeply
Surrounded inner sounds
Soliciting feverishly
Desires embedded deeply
Inadequate uncertainty
If I could just be hungry

Hungry
Grinding indefinitely
Consuming optimistically
Drowning circumspectly
Greed obviously
Believing lies willingly
If I could just be hungry

ONLY Guarantee

Every so often I go through these phases.
About all the times I complained about,
Not always willing to accept
What God protected me from
Mortality seems so far from me
So I have this false belief that I control destiny
Always see death thinking it won't happen to me
In life that's the ONLY guarantee.

Everything is a what if,
Unknown reasons have me in disbelief
That this is where I'm supposed to be
As if one, two or even three
Previous decisions would make a better me
As if there is ONE of the billions of people
That does not have a single problem
As if there is one decision for the ONE of billions that could
have solved them
We are all on the same destiny The ONLY guarantee

Waking up grateful for where I am at today.
Making a choice for peace in my own way
Learning to become more resilient
Seeking patience in what I do
Just accepting what I have been through

There is always more to do
But important to realize
There's a limit to random things to do
Spending time on so many things
But do they lead to any generational things
How will the seed not even planted
Benefit from where you are standing
No matter how much it's decorated
Along the way there is finality,
The ONLY guarantee.

First

First month of the year
Barely finished last year
Just watched time tick away
Pretending I'm new today
Like I won't go home the same way

First day of the month
Frost in every window
Cold settled in
Wind knocking on the door
Looking for more

FATHERLESS | The Evolution

First hour of the day
Trying to end yesterday
Sleep keeps evading me
Changing the past
Into what if fantasies

First minute of the hour
Something about seeing those zeros
Always gives me power
Optimistically what does this mean to me
Feeling so desperately

First second of the minute
What should I do
Counting down to inevitability
Why do we act so pleasantly
Feeling it leave slowly

Sy Bryant

Releasing This Pain

Releasing this pain
The shadow of insanity
It's staring back at me
Deciphering the past
After action reviews
Fishbones and 5-Whys
Nothing comes through

Releasing this pain
But how'd I get here
Could not predict this
Feeling like a sickness
Prevailing inside of me
Ain't no medicine
No form of therapy

Releasing this pain
At the next sun rise
Just tired of sinking inside
Shoulders too worn out
Can no longer hold out
World pressing me
Down on both knees

FATHERLESS | The Evolution

Releasing this pain
Shedding the deadness
Tortured and bruised
Need perseverance
Time to stand up
Got to get up
Fulfill this destiny
Let shine that God in me

FATHERLESS - The Perpetuation

We will all go through that moment of awakening. Regardless of how long ago the negativity was conceived. Regardless of when we realized it inadvertently became ingrained in our life. Regardless of how damning it felt, once we evolve into a new way of thinking and being. It is our responsibility to perpetuate a new way of thinking. Leveraging Hope, Faith, Love and Patience to lead our life evermore.

Breathe

Inhaling from the inside out
Longing refreshment
Chilled air warmed soul
Deeply deeply breathe

Life's curious ways
Anxiety driven passion
Exhale relaxing satisfaction
Deeply deeply breathe

Winding to conclusion
Slower repetition
Subtle warmness
Deeply deeply breathe

Chasing

Chasing, endlessly pursuing
Wanting elusive things aloft beings
Experiences unmet
Energy spent wanting

Chasing, constantly waiting
Hoping for a different outcome
Feelings damaged
Faith diminished

Chasing, patiently seeing
Living a tumultuous fantasy
Life wasting
Laugh gone

Chasing, new reality
Looking, new paths revealed
Patiently waiting
Pleasing satisfaction

Following Sunshine

Following sunshine
Early morning stretch
Reaching to the depths haven't even started yet
So I take a deep breath
Not sure what I have left
Nothing short of miraculous
Heart so gracious

Following sunshine
Everything on my mind is mine
Thankful for everything in me
Now I'm wondering why me, So I take a deep breath
Accepting world as I see it
Not sure if I believe it
Mindful intent

Following sunshine
Not a cloud in the sky
Seeing the full horizon
Life is not surprising
So I take a deep breath
Knowing that clouds come and go
Regardless of the sky
I got to keep moving by

Following sunshine
Sun approaching the end
Darkest shadow creeps in
Doing my best to object
With endless energy I'm begging for synergy
Integrating light and death
Relishing in faith and opportunity

Speak Life.

Speak Life.
Amen.
Start each day with an Amen.
No vain shit about my eyes open and I can breathe.
My life ain't for me, it's for the seeds to breathe.

Speak Life.
Energy.
Putting in that energy.
Solid work for every minute with the seeds.
Opening their minds to the possibility of the seed.

Speak Life.
Patience.
Avoid even saying Patience.

No time to wait for everything to be perfectly aligned.
That focus is driven to succeed relentlessly aligned.

Speak Life.
Persevere.
Always persevere.
No need to stop when the destination is so clear.
Hustling through adversity makes life clear.

Connected Belief

Pure openness
Sincere relief
Bonded indefinitely
Tried necessities
Connected belief

Pure joy
Sincere empathy
Bonded infinity
Tried purposely
Connected belief

Pure understanding
Sincere compassion

Bonded perpetually
Tried ambitiously
Connected belief

Pure sensitivity
Sincere charity
Bonded endlessly
Tried earnestly
Connected belief

Creating Abundantly

Creating my own reality
Exhausted living in fantasy
Tangibly holding on
Been dreaming for too long
Spontaneously making
Dreams into reality

Stay living abundantly
Endlessly breathing this air
Constantly consuming H_2O
This earth provides everything
There is nothing more that I need

FATHERLESS | The Perpetuation

Only thing I can give is this seed

Enjoying every single day
Screaming congratulations
Just because I've seen the sun today
Excited at the possibility
For what the world has for me
Feeling the greatness destiny

Happiness each and every day
Grateful to be alive today
Take a deep sigh just to release
Any pressure bearing down on me
Looking to the sky optimistically
Digesting every blessings eternally

Void of Doubt

Suddenly without any feeling
Is this the peace they talk about
Pure emptiness void of doubt
Existing on nothing
Mind is at ease
Peace

Hearing every sound
Within a mile around
Hearing beauty
In every unique thing
Even the subtleties of the wind
Peace

Finally feel the things you say
It's like snow fall on a pure day
Quietness has engulfed me
 Able to be right where I am
To feel the world about me
Peace

FATHERLESS | The Perpetuation

Laid down to sleep
Joy blessing me
Thankfully existing
With the purest energy
Embracing whatever change may be
Peace

Believe with me

Doubt is a curse
It only focuses on the worst
Just asking that you
Believe with me
You are everything
That God made you to be
Doing that grown shit
On your own shit

Fear is a mind killer
Limiting our possibilities
Just need you to
Believe with me
Anything is feasible
Just walk this with me
Your greatness materializing

FATHERLESS | The Perpetuation

Even in small material things

Hope is our destiny
Opening our hearts to joy
Just want you to Believe with me
Arms open wide
Scream that desire with pride
The anointments received
Expressing these blessings

Faith is our way
Shining toward a greater day
Just feel this and
Believe with me
Happiness resounding
Our hearts stay pounding
Blessed through glorious things.

To Me

Swear God be talking to me
Showing me little things
Seeing it in big ways
Every single opportunity
I know it's all God's way
Humbly I ask constantly
For more strength
When I know
There is nothing in me
And I become hesitant

Swear God be talking to me
Just in everything I do
Feeling outside energy
Straight through me
Gaining spiritual
Remnant of the beginning
First humans just being
Accepting every learning
As if I'm their meaning
And all those lives was for a meaning

Swear God be talking to me
Granting every dream
Before I even wish for it

FATHERLESS | The Perpetuation

Answer each prayer
As if I deserve any of it
Gratefully accepting it
I stopped asking why me
Learning to let God do for me
And I'm believing in
Every bit of God's energy

Swear God be talking to me
Left foot, right foot
Keep walking steady
As long as I follow orders
I'll have heaven for an eternity
Patiently walking circumspectly
Never doubting the path
Laid out right before me
Everything is left for me
Bowing to that God in me

What It Seems

Not sure what to do with this emotion
Wallo reminded me about expectation
Here I am doing what I tell others not to
Thinking how'd I get to a place where it got to
Feeling so unappreciative in all this
Just that deep pondering that I miss

Accepting envy from the TV
Creating unrealistic moments of fantasy
Mind repetitively reminding me
All this was initiated by me
Afraid to contemplate the true meaning
Knowing the outcome is demeaning

Avoiding every truth, I see
Instead of managing what could be
Trying to ignore everything that could be
Just trying to reach a state of peace
If I could just stop thinking of the increase
Know it ain't right but I need that release

The future is too far to be seen
Focused on the past in what it should have been
Missing out on every present opportunity
Then expecting peace when I'm sleepy

Sy Bryant   149

The impossible creation of these dreams
Closer than what it seems

Show Strength

Show strength
Through every weakness
Accepting that I am
Everything that I have done
Molded through hardship Into what I've become

Show strength
Through every tear
Releasing all I fear
Uncontrollable circumstances
Finding fake comfort loving fake romances

Show strength
Through the Earth's rotation
Defensively approaching situations
The past me, has gripped me
Presently not focused on me
Praying seeds are blessed irrespectively

Show strength
Through every heartbreak
Accepting quickly it's for my sake
Holding onto a finite being
Prevents realization of the dream
Reaching toward that infinite being

This Is The Reality

This is the reality
The majority of my time I spend on other's lives
Leveraging everything family given
And I give to others
Freely and completely
Give it, like I received it
Without expectation of anything

This is the reality raised with a different view
Expectations were too high
To ever be close to failure
Now I struggle with anyone
That intentionally wants failure
Pushing feverishly
Until others can see their own destiny

This is the reality
I don't give a fuck about anything
Literally could stand up and walk out,
And never return
Embedded from my legacy
Selfishly I only think about me
When it is no longer satisfying
To help you see the truth...

Untouchable Reality

Getting higher on some different shit
It's from all the difficult shit
That fuck it shit
It made me stronger than I am physically
Leaping cross chasms cold and dingy
It's just that untouchable reality.

When I found out what God created for me
It no longer mattered that my daddy left me
Everything got to focus on the people around me
Diligently savage, articulately ravage, violently
I use it for power insatiability
It's just that untouchable reality.

FATHERLESS | The Perpetuation

Sanity is Kryptonite on a lonely night
It's the pain I lavish every night
Fuels the paramount of that full moon night
Face gritted up, pondering strangers mentally
Pockets empty miss that job I pimped easily
It's just that untouchable reality.

Sigh For A Smile

Sigh for a smile
Remembering when I
Would sigh out of frustration
As an emotional release
Opening the valve
Releasing it all
Emptying my cup
Vulnerabilities and all

Sigh for a smile
Recognizing every trouble
Each and every trial I've been through
The tribulations that weakened me
Somehow ended up
Strengthened me
Lavishing in all of it

FATHERLESS | The Perpetuation

Because I am all of it

Sigh for a smile
Remembering the many days
When I thought
There was no other way
Holding onto the past
Cause the present
Wasn't what I planned
Now I see the real plan

Sigh for a smile
When I lay my head
Down to sleep
Everything I am
Is what you expected of me
Never relinquish peace Or serenity
The alignment to destiny

Sigh for a smile
Shaking my head
In the amount of disbelief
Remembering those that fell
Acknowledging those enslaved
Calling out to the lost
And it's just by chance
I am not the same

Focusing

Focusing on me
Reflecting internally
Closing every door
Opening every window
Filtering all contact
Allowing myself
To reconnect
With the only one
I have to face every day
Me.

Focusing on me
Foreign as it sounds
Creating a time
For me to fellowship with me
Permitting my anxiety
Avoiding distractions
With every intent
Not to respond
To only have attention on
Me.

Focusing on me
I am a stranger
Developed independently

FATHERLESS | The Perpetuation

There was no room for me
This life, a sacrifice
Giving continually
Every seed planted
Every water dropped
Provide endlessly
Just not for
Me

Focusing on me
As if I need permission
Dreams so long lost
Mindfulness in the wilderness
Casket Closing into a final state
People praising feelings
From shared interactions
Granting tears
For past and future years
Finally seeing
Me

Thoughts

Sun rising through the clouds
It feels so loud
Hiding my eyes
From this beautiful sunshine
Don't even know the time
Deeply breathing
Crisp air is relieving
It's purity
Fueling me

Fueling me
With all its energy
Metaphorically transcendent
Rising up the mountain high
Objectively choosing steps
Going for the highest high
Blindly following faith
Stand ready and braced
Guiding me without a trace

Guiding me without a trace
Thanking God for the grace
From this precious seed
Did I survive, destined to survive
Seeing so many fall

Sy Bryant   157

It's why I'm here standing tall
In the prudence of hope
On the last rope

On the last rope
Speak with conviction
Winning wasn't my intention
Just the evidence of ascension
Cannot remember every step
Put every effort into every step
Now I'm at the end of this
Six feet under all of it

Moment

Existing in this moment
Lost for a moment
Forget every moment
That I loved for a moment

Slowly crying out this fear
So tired of this fear
Avoiding life in fear
Losing everything through fear

Understanding every time
That I wasted so much time
Remember counting each time
That I lost every time

Slowly see things differently
Shall I contemplate differently
Life hitting me differently
Resurrecting new beginnings differently

Existing in Earth's moment
Breathing but a moment
Feeling every moment
Loved that moment

Moving Past It All

Moving past it all
Periodically I give it my all
Focusing on new seeds planted
The challenge to endure
The foundation that was laid
Thankful for every lesson
It wasn't until my 3rd decade
That I truly learned manhood

FATHERLESS | The Perpetuation

Up until that point I was just angry
Did well though
So people thought I was good.

Moving past it all
It's hard to relax the energy
Nothing positive from it
Just accustomed to it
There is comfort in this
This potential energy
Always ready to explode
And just so easy
With the fanatical memories
Peace of mind
It's so far outta reach
Years of writing
Still no release

Moving past it all
On a good day
I can avoid and recall it all
Each of those moments
That defines who I am
Sheltered, Loyal, Dogmatic
The shelter is the comfort
Enjoy it profusely
Loyalty embedded
Until you cross me

FATHERLESS | The Perpetuation

Dogmatic to an Atomic tune
Un-relinquishing pursuit
Whatever I do

Moving past it all
Ironically afraid to even say
I'd change it all
I know enough to know
Life isn't perfect at all
Everyone has success
And everyone will fall
We all get to the same point In the very end
We are laid out
Or in a lump of ash
Left to face our true sins
The triumphs and the disasters

That Is Life

Eyes are focused on the door
Expecting to hear footsteps
Left in a dismal space
Never know what's next
Endlessly expecting
Something different
Imagination controlling
Every breath

Ears focused on the meaning
Each and every sound
Believing what is said
Keeps me above ground
Words differing
From action's reactions
Left with nothing
Life's satisfaction

Nose controlled by that aroma
Breathing deeply
Not willing to admit
What's wrong with me
Revolution of imperfection
Paralyzed by reflections
What's left in me

FATHERLESS | The Perpetuation

These sins are deadly

Mind racing to end this
No one would ever
Even believe this
Captivated desires
Prioritized evil fires
Climbing into abyss
Looking back
Damn I missed

This New Day

Opening my eyes to this new day
Same ol dark ways
See life from a different view
Based on the things I been through
Was never taught To worship Santa Clause
 I was taught to be Chris Kringle
Be the Peace and the Joy
That everyone is into

Opening the curtains to this new day
Everything still in its own way
Beauty of every single thing
The greenness of life
The blooming flowers
Right in front of me
Humbled by every mercy
Even when I'm down on my knees
The spirit swells inside of me

Opening the door to this new day
Songs repetitively repeating for me
Warmth warming me
Brightness shining for me
Invisible feeling passed by me
Hard to be egotistical

FATHERLESS | The Perpetuation

Hard to stay humble
When all this opportunity
Right in front of me

Realizing the realness of this new day
It never has to end
It's meant to exist perpetually
Without hesitation
Counting down to the last
Aggressively pursuing
Each and every moment
Cause at any moment.......It'll be th.....

FATHERLESS - The Redemption

This pursuit of written word died right after High School. From that point to now, feelings, events, illogical behavior festered within me. Controlling the ability to trust in others or to simply believe someone at their word. Fortunately, friends and in-laws existed in my life to provide a guiding light in the most desperate of situations. There was no one to repair the holes, then I realized, that was for me to do. Writing provided a way out. Past every decision made, for me or against me. Ending every tear that washed away hope, I am finally free. The Redemption is Here.

Compilation

It's like
I feel like
I am a compilation
Of each man that was in my life
But none of them
Would ever get along
Let alone be around each other
So these divergent feelings
Rip at my conscience
Unable to process reality
Escaped each opportunity
Someone suggested
Psychological therapy
Unable to bypass the stigma
That mental health
Is synonymous with sanity
Staying unresolved
Nothing is solved

It's like
I feel like
Pieces of the past
That I hold onto
Were the worst
Possible scenarios

FATHERLESS | The Redemption

Unable to see positivity
And each laugh
Grounded in throbbing persecution
The best days
Are downpours
That warm rain
Hiding the distinguishing factors
Stuck between tears
And the thunderous agony
Lightning lighting a way
If only,
if only,
if only,
I could focus long enough
To stay on track
These complicating views
Stay pulling me back

It's like
I feel like
I can see the sunrise
At that moment
When that shine
Shines on me
And I'm silently
Just trying to be me
Birds reminding me
Earth's natural beauty

Sy Bryant   168

FATHERLESS | The Redemption

Arms outstretched
Absorbing that vitamin D
Before the world
Takes hold of me
Inside each microprocessor
Activated by history
Trying to predict
Every step of my destiny
Without repeating
Any step of their reality
Ending opportunities
Before they even begin
Immovable the greatest sin
Life is living for me
Buried alive
I won't survive
Strong roots
No tree

From Day One

From day one
I rejected you
Self-inflicted this way
Before you even settled
Already concluded your departure
Lost so many chances
Missed the opportunities
To learn and grow together

From day one
I knew I wasn't the focus
Seeking my mother's attention
But that was my attention
Didn't want to share
What I had rightfully stole
Wasn't willing to negotiate
Opened the Art of War

From day one
Relentless in pursuit
Battling endlessly
No one was taking
Her from me
Creating insurmountable obstacles
But possession being the 9/10

FATHERLESS | The Redemption

I struggled for the win

From day one
Every visit was contentious
Until you opened up independently
And started teaching new things
Applying castling, running wires, sheetrock
Just basic things
Filling every void and gap
Wish I had you back

From day one
To that very last day
Half my life passed away
Finding comfort in your peace
Eternally grateful you chose me
Not every person is able
Or even willing to
Care for another's seed

Unknowingly

Unknowingly
Entered into a different state of mind
What if your words were true
And life would be worse
Knowing and loving you
And everything
And everybody
That I hold close to me
Wouldn't even know me
Desperately grasping
At every possible timeline
Not sure which one is mine

Unknowingly
Gladly provide forgiveness
Speak though all the treachery
The reality knows me differently
Holding onto emptiness
Fostering hateful thoughts
Just to unleash them willingly
To any hateful human being
Transposing everything about you
Literally to them
There will be no remorse
Not even hesitation of thought

FATHERLESS | The Redemption

Unknowingly
Provide you control
It was amplified
By every single being
Promising beliefs I needed
Gullible the first time
Open minded to a cure
I know your name
But I will never say it
My seeds will never know you
Not having you abandoned them
Like I know you would do

Unknowingly
Persevering every opportunity
End the cycle of a father leaving
The men in my paternal lineage
Just did it so routinely
Dropping seeds quickly
Stay around long enough
Just in time to germinate
Never see the fruit of the labor
Never know if I'm really of you
I don't even know you

This Is It

This is the meaning
This is the solution
This is the feeling
This is it

This is that groove
This is that victory
This is that success
This is it

This is the reason
This is why
This is meant to be
This is it

Grief

Midst of the grief
Fighting the belief
Everything has its place
So must this reality in my face
Pulling at me
With every single breath
Waking with tears
My own dreams
Perpetuating fears

Deep into grief
Asking questions rhetorically
Only God can answer me
Knees bended
Screaming to remain sane
Replaying each scene
Was it meant to be me
Not accepting this destiny
Fire keeps growing in me
Afraid to sleep

Alone in this grief
Every grief opening
Every single time I felt this
Appreciating lessons

FATHERLESS | The Redemption

Some told remain old
Expecting something different
Hard to bear this
Praying for something
Not even sure what yet

Buried in grief
Flowing through me
Essence of everything
Innocence was fleeting
Unable to protect me
Envied each day dream
Thinking I'd be free
I changed locations
Escaped reality
But it never left me

Family

Faint memories
Devastated me
The fallacy of belief
Holding onto fiction
Artistically describing
Each and every interaction
Remembering Christmas morning
Thinking we were a family

Haunted memories
Seeing who made you
Each time I thought
Even for an instance
The other half of me
Finally wanted me
Just an illusion I created
Wanting family

Fake Memories
Created multi parent household
Lasted until I was 10 years old
Held me and allowed me to grow
Didn't even know
Parents weren't supposed to go
Slowly realized

FATHERLESS | The Redemption

The one sided family

Angered memories
Woke up realizing
Single parent household
Faults amplified
The rejection taken hold
Half of what made me
No longer wanted me
That's my family

Ignored memories
Siblings visited
Far off and distant
Never an embrace
Barely a hello
Realized, for the first time
I was alone
Abandoned by family

Eventuality

Seeing you lying there
Unwilling to accept reality
Life wasn't intended to be fair
Endless cycle of the
Earth's core
Shuffling us endlessly
We all have one common
Eventuality

Hearing youth refer casually
Lack of Mr., lack of Sir
First name commonality
Exiting life so freely
Narcotics and alcohol
Compounded routinely
Eventuality

The latest story
Heard it so clearly
Confronted on the block
Using loaned narcotics
Avoiding the crack commandments
Outcome predetermined
Eventuality

FATHERLESS | The Redemption

Owing large revenue
Nothing in hand
Nothing else to do
Archaic methods applied
Upon the torso and head
Ignoring what's next
Eventuality

Sobering moment
Knowing consent was given
No more life within
Holding to every promise lost
Grasping laugh of the past
Accepting reality
Eventuality

Recalling instances
When laughter filled me
Fueled off of your very energy
Cannot fathom what led you astray
Thought the love was sincere
If it was, you would still be here
Eventuality

Kept Thinking

Kept thinking
I could escape my past
Find a way to end the wrath
I thought the longer I lived
The more happiness I would have
And old painful things
Would fall away at last

Wanted to believe in pure things
That not everyone is an enemy
But had too many trusted faces
That I can no longer tell
Who is who In the fell clutch of circumstance
No longer willing to take a chance

Kept thinking
Loss is only temporary
And eventually it is replaced
In some type of way
Replenishing what was missing
When protection is lost
A different person emerges

Wanted to believe in pure things
That this evil festering is temporary

FATHERLESS | The Redemption

Now we are so intertwined
I smile so you believe I'm fine
Ruthlessly divert conversations
Protecting everything left in me
Barely holding the vengeance within

Kept thinking
If I had that day again
If my God created protector
Was just there
But he never showed up
And never will again …. Crushed into oblivion

Pieces of Me

Feeling like
I've been pulled together
Randomly
The father and mother are clear
But he was never here
Now I think back unraveling
Each layer of me that I see
Seeing every man
That somehow made
An impression on me

Learned love at a very early age
Remembering those hugs
You loved me like
I Never made a single mistake
For whatever reason
You only came around on holidays
Only found out your hidden identity
When AIDS took you away

Learned how to manifest anger
It was routinely on display
Cannot remember my age
But I knew it was in second grade
It reminds me

FATHERLESS | The Redemption

Of one of those superhero characters
You won't like when they angry
Because in hindsight
I cannot fathom
What a classroom of 2nd graders
Could ever do to make you break a chalkboard
But I learned to hold shit in
And when my seeds messed up I let it explode
Again and Again and Again

Learned how to ride or die
Nothing special
It was just the look in your eyes
Revenge is a bitter pill
Sometimes you get so deep in it
There's no way out of it
That's why you need
To have heat with you
Because badge or not
No one wants to get shot
Always stay ready
With a plan to enter
A plan to escape
But if you get stuck
Shut the fuck up
Let the lawyer plead your case

FATHERLESS | The Redemption

Learned how to just cut ties
Give it your all
Until you bust
Then walk away
With no hesitancy
Nothing means everything
Even though I was your seed
The gravity of you leaving
Helped me leave everything

Learned a lot of things randomly
Watching life's sermons
While people speaking eloquently
Seeing every addiction
Removed every narcotic curiosity
Regardless of the need to escape
When that high wore off
There is nowhere left to escape
And the reality of who you are
That is all that's left
Accepting who you really are
Until your final last breath

Learned by watching more than hearing
Seeing you fix things
Instead of using yellow pages
Seeing the logic
Was no internet on site

FATHERLESS | The Redemption

Laying tiles without a single mistake
Hanging Sheetrock with one hand
Hammer it in with the other hand
Realizing desire more important
Than impossibility
When you want something done
Waiting on someone
Ain't always In your reach

Pieces together
Feeling like those old scarecrows
Resembling something real
But in reality
Just the manifestation
Of different realities
And none of them fit together
Always challenged for them
To work together
Even if all those influencers
Were in the same room
They wouldn't like each other
Yet I'm perpetuating their ideals
Stuck not knowing how to feel
Unwilling to let them go
Selfishly it's all I know

Manifested

Say the word it's reality
Managing the manifestation
Of simple childhood wishes
Managing the manifestation
Of adolescent dreams
Managing the manifestation
Of new entry goals
Managing the manifestation
Of mid-life crisis
Managing the manifestation
Of grandchildren licenses
Managing the manifestation
Of being 6 feet under

Speaking powerfully with no control
Couldn't control the time
Couldn't control the place
Yet I still spoke with powerful grace

All the things I've asked for came to pass
At the end I'm still in this wooden box
In a concrete case
With 283 cubes of dirt on my face.

Could never just be in the moment,

so I lost every moment I lived.
Always manifesting toward the future,
missing every gift from the present.
In the end.
It's just the end.
Got everything I wanted.
I still have nothing.

Everything

Everything I used to believe
Believe in ideas that made everything work
Work that ensured we were safe
Safe enough to realize future success
Success that transposed our biggest dreams
Dreams involving strong family
Family enduring and supporting wild things
Things that inspired us, enlightened us to fantasy
Fantasy driving our ruthless pursuit of anything
Anything that matters.
Anything that builds
Builds the best of us to continue loving trust
Trust that no matter what we are everything.

Silent Night

Deep into the solitude of the dark night
Listening intently to the silence of thought
Lost dreams resurrect reminiscence of light

Looking clearly into the darkness
Hoping for a day that will never be, hoping to be free
The derivative of constant peril

Heart beat's deafening sound in the abyss
Praying for solitude, wishing for peace.
Silent night, searching for increase

Ride

Ride..... As far as possible.
There is no time or speed quest.
Just a feeling of emptiness.
Striving to have a mind clear of any premeditated thought.
Focused on spiritual oneness,
Aligning the mind to push the body past what it was taught.

Ride.....Far away.
Up a hill I know I cannot climb.
Chasing down the speeders staying right on their line.
Reaching eagerly for that point of exhaustion.
Pushing relentlessly until there is nothing left,
But the will to say hold on.

Ride.... Far into.
Into that bliss of nothingness where no one exists.
Just having hydrating liquids as my only salvation.
Feeling that physicalness. Muscles tightening.
All the while I get stronger and stronger.
There is nothing close to the spiritual awakening,
than challenging yourself beyond your own beliefs.

Ride .... Ride out of.
Out of the limits of this world. Into this euphoria of oneness
with nothingness.

Living Today

Ever felt like everything we believed was a lie
It's like we realize now everything is real,
But you were living in a fantasy, not reality.
Now the reality that we see
Ain't what we expected it to be.

Ever thought what if we changed that one decision in our life.
It's like we associate our entire existence to one moment in time.
But that time is long gone and so now all we try to do is hold on.

Ever believed there is something better in this world.
Something inspiring,
Something serene,
Something that makes this insane world livable.
Something to wake up for.
There just has to be more.

Ever thought about the future.
And realized everything in our future doesn't exist in our present.
Ever realize that we just created another fantasy,
Instead of living today.

Wrong Expectations

Maintaining the wrong expectations
Forcing myself into beliefs
Believing that everyone always strives to improve
Believing that everybody wants more in life
Believing that we all know we need to know more

Loving the wrong expectations
Forcing myself into attractions
Thinking that beauty equates to personality
Thinking memorization is the same as intelligence
Thinking good thought leads to good action

Realizing the wrong expectations
Forcing myself into realism
Hoping that I accept what is right in front of me
Hoping that I do all I can do without you
Hoping that this is all just a dream and peace is peaceful

Truth

Exhale the deep release,
Days tread,
Serene peace,
Anticipating special places
Bracing for the sudden paces

Traversing raves
Endless waves
Silent movement
Gently sent

Inhale the pollution
Painfully offered solution
Death so close auras release

Motion halts
Heart assaults
Despair engulfs
Freedom Lost

Starts With Me

Staring into this subtle breeze
Continuous cloud blocking the burning sun
Endless green filling up the remaining scene
Left to wonder and understand this new summer.

Thinking through these constant obligations
Payments, commitments, deadlines, no time
Every single day, less than 24 hours left
Each and every day 48 hours of things left

In this crazy phase, not focused on anything
Somehow floating in this hazy daze of everything
Feeling empty, peacefully, breathing evenly
Something familiar within this space

Watching the sky move, while the bugs bite
Life's little annoyances, keeping me attentive
The daydreams of a fantasy of what-if realities
Approaching closely serenity and it all starts with me

One Day

One day, there will be a day for me.
This day, I won't be subject to false totality.
This day, time is created for my own selfish pleasures.
This day, I will be so high no one can see.
This day surrounded by beautiful warm waters of the sea.

One day, there will be a day for me.
This day, no one will ask me for a thing.
This day, the world will be at my beckoning.
This day, time will have no bound.
This day, I can only hear beautiful sound.

One day, there will be a day for me.
This day, I could walk on beaches endlessly.
This day, my appetite is quenched.
This day, my mind is free.
This day, is just for me.

Chaotic

Life's simple phrases cause diluted faces.
Making crazy thoughts real, making me feel.
Can I feel free?
Can I see something to feel?
These crazy thoughts are betraying my sanity.
Life's pleasant season is my only reason.
Staying in this chaotic world.

If things were real we would all see the same thing in the
same way.
This perceived world has so many fake pearls,
in the beholder's eyes,
I behold more lies.
I've seen my whole life in an unforeseen way.
Making sure I manage in this chaotic world.

When I realized the sun never does rise.
And I'm walking as a microorganism of infinite wisdom.
Talking through doors avoiding whores.
Listening to the moon's light as the world goes into death's
foyer.
In this chaos,
I only see the chaotic chaos.

Child Is Born

Since I realized I was alone.
Since I realized he was never coming home.
Accepting the loss within me.
Learning everything independently.
There were always others around me.
But none of them looked like me.

Inherited love's independent feeling.
Embedded in the concept of creation.
Complicated in that new beginning.
Proudly smiling at the planted seed.
The proud excitement of something new.
Anticipating loving you.

Wrote down every promise.
Each and every action I pledged to keep.
Looking retrospectively.
Mirror gave me all that I needed.
Every gap and hole in me.
Providing every opportunity

That day finally arrived.
Wish I could have captured that tear from my eye.
That love anew.
Never knew love.

FATHERLESS | The Redemption

Like I knew it with you.

Conception of history.
Realization of everything in me.
Damnation struck me down.
Evolution couldn't stop this now.
Perpetuation of something renewed.
Redemption of this crown.
My life is now sworn.
My child is born.